Contents

Rain or shine?

When you wake up in the morning, do you look out of the window and say, "What's the weather like today?"

Maybe it's cloudy and wet, or hot and sunny. The wind might be blowing or perhaps it's freezing cold.

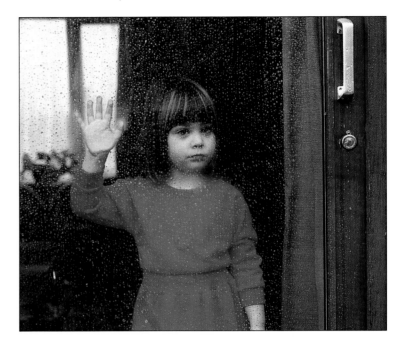

What would the weather need to be like if you wanted to use any of these things?

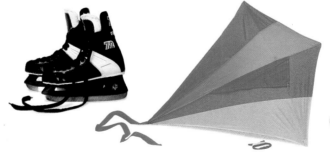

💡 THINK ABOUT IT!

What is your favourite kind of weather? Imagine what it would be like if it was your favourite kind of weather every day!

IT'S SCIENCE!

Weather

Sally Hewitt

W

FRANKLIN WATTS

NEW YORK • LONDON • SYDNEY

First published in 1999 by Franklin Watts
96 Leonard Street, London EC2A 4XD

Franklin Watts Australia
14 Mars Road
Lane Cove
NSW 2066

Series editor: Rachel Cooke
Designer: Mo Choy
Consultant: Sally Nankivell-Aston
Photography: Ray Moller unless otherwise acknowledged
Picture research: Sue Mennell

A CIP catalogue record for this book
is available from the British Library.

ISBN 0 7496 3323 9

Dewey Classification 551.5

Printed in Malaysia

Acknowledgements:
Bubbles p. 6tr (Ian West); Bruce Coleman pp. 11tr (Brian Henderson), 16bl (Thomas Buchholz), 21tr (William S. Paton),
21br (Norbert Schwirtz), 24tr (Andrew Davies); © Crown p. 26br; FLPA p. 20b (Eric and David Hosking);
Robert Harding pp. 20t (Caroline Wood); Holt Studios International p. 15tl (Ivor Speed);
Image Bank pp. 9tl (John P. Kelly), 11tl (P. Ploquin), 12tl (Pete Turner) 13bl, 14t (Mitchell Funk), 14b (Nancy Brown), 22
(Pete Turner), 23b (A. T. Willett), 24br (Joseph van Os), 25tr (Yellow Dog Productions); Images Colour Library pp. 9tr, 19, 21l, 27tl;
Impact Photos p. 18l (Paul Forster); Science Photo Library p. 26tr (Damien Lovegrove); Still Pictures pp. 23t (Gerard and
Margi Moss), 26bl (Dera); Telegraph Colour Library pp. 10t, 25br (Bluestone Productions).
Thanks, too, to our models: Natimi & Shalika Black-Heaven, Jack Mitchell, Shauna Morris and Erin Bhogal.

We wear special clothes for different kinds of weather.

Waterproof clothes help to keep us dry in the rain. Light clothes keep us cool on a hot day and thick clothes keep us warm on a cold day.

TRY IT OUT!

Collect together some of your clothes. Sort them into clothes to wear on a hot day, clothes for a cold day and clothes for a wet day. Do you know what the clothes are made of?

7

Hot and cold

One of the things we want to know when we ask "What's the weather like today?" is how hot or cold it is. We call this the **temperature**.

Hot, cold, freezing, chilly, boiling and cool are some words we use to describe how the temperature makes us feel. Can you think of some more temperature words?

THINK ABOUT IT!

What's the weather like during summer and winter? Which has hot temperatures? Which has cold temperatures?

LOOK AGAIN

Look again at page 7 to find some clothes you might wear in the summer and some clothes for the winter.

We measure **air** temperature in degrees Centigrade (°C) with a **thermometer**.

When the temperature drops below 0 °C puddles freeze and you may see frost or even snow.

It feels very hot when the temperature rises above 30 °C.

 TRY IT OUT!

If you have a thermometer, hang it outside in the shade above the ground and check the temperature daily. How does the temperature make you feel? What do you need to wear?

9

Sunshine

Do you like warm sunny days when there are no **clouds** and the sky is blue? You probably say, "What a lovely day!" when the sun shines.

 LOOK AGAIN

Look again at page 6 to find something you might do on a warm sunny day.

The sun warms the ground and then heat from the ground warms the air above it.

During the night, the ground cools down again. This makes the air cooler in the mornings even on a sunny day.

 TRY IT OUT!

On a sunny day go outside and feel the ground. Does it feel warm? Feel earth, stone, grass and any other different kinds of ground you can find. Which feels the warmest?

The weather over many **deserts** is hot and dry; it hardly ever changes. Plants and animals have to live with very little water.

Cactus plants keep a store of water in their fleshy stems. Animals come out at night when it is cooler.

 THINK ABOUT IT!

What do you think would happen if it was very hot and sunny every day where you live?

 SAFETY WARNING!

On sunny days, wear a hat and sun cream to protect you from the hot rays of the sun. Never look straight at the sun.

Air

Our planet Earth is wrapped around by a layer of air called the **atmosphere**.

The atmosphere protects Earth from the fierce heat and dangerous rays of the sun. The atmosphere also helps to keep Earth warm.

Clouds and tiny droplets of water in the atmosphere work like a blanket. They help to stop warmth from the sun moving back into space.

 LOOK AGAIN

Look again at page 10 to find how the air is heated up.

 THINK ABOUT IT!

Out in space where there is no air, there is no weather!

You can't see air but you can feel it. Wind is moving air. You can feel wind on your skin and blowing your hair. You can feel whether the air is hot or cold.

 TRY IT OUT!

Go outside. Can you feel the air moving?
Is it moving a lot or just a little?
Does the air feel hot or cold?

Air is thickest nearer to the ground. This is where it moves around and changes the weather, causing cloud, wind and rain.

High above the clouds the air is thinner. Aeroplanes often fly in the sunshine high above the clouds where they are not so likely to be bumped around by rough weather.

13

Wind

When air moves you can feel it as wind. You can't see the wind, but you can see what it does.

The wind moves air from one place to another. Winds from cold places bring cold air. Winds from warm places bring warm air.

Wind blows clouds across the sky. Tree branches bend and flags flap in the wind. What else could you see that would tell you it was a windy day?

 **LOOK AGAIN**

Look again at page 6 for something to do on a windy day.

Wind may be gentle or fierce enough to blow down a tree.

A scarf blowing in the wind tells you which direction the wind is coming from.

 TRY IT OUT!

Make some wind chimes to measure the strength of the wind. Cut about 8 fairly wide strips of foil. Thread cotton onto the end of each strip. Slightly crumple the foil. Tie all the cotton threads together and hang the foil strips in a window. They will rustle together gently in a breeze and wave around and rattle noisily in a strong wind – the louder the noise, the stronger the wind.

 THINK ABOUT IT!

Why might someone need to know the direction and strength of the wind?

15

Clouds

When the sun heats up the ground, the ground heats the air above it. Warm air rises because it is lighter than cold air.

 TRY IT OUT!

Watch warm air rising by blowing up a balloon and hanging it above a radiator. The radiator heats the air in and around the balloon. The balloon will float up with the rising warm air around the radiator.

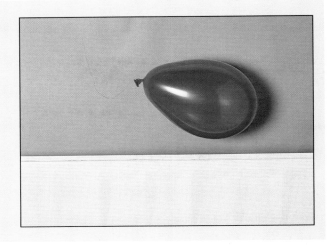

When warm air rises it cools down in the colder air higher up. As it cools, an invisible gas in the air called **water vapour** turns into droplets of water. These droplets collect together and become a cloud.

Mist is really a cloud very near the ground. Walking in the mist is like walking through a cloud.

cirrus

cumulonimbus

stratus

cumulus

Clouds of different shapes tell us what kind of weather is on its way.

Cirrus clouds floating high in blue skies warn that the weather is about to change.

Giant **cumulonimbus** clouds bring storms.

You can see small, white fluffy **cumulus** clouds in good weather.

Low layers of very dark **stratus** clouds bring rain.

 TRY IT OUT!

Look up at the sky and see if you can tell what kind of weather the clouds will bring.

LOOK AGAIN

Look again at page 14 to find what moves clouds across the sky.

Rain

Rain clouds are full of tiny droplets of water or tiny **ice crystals**. Slowly these droplets stick together. They become too big and heavy to stay in the clouds and fall as rain.

Light rain or drizzle hardly makes you wet.

You'll need an umbrella in heavy rain.

You have to run for shelter to keep dry in a downpour!

 TRY IT OUT!

Cut the top off a plastic bottle, turn it upside-down and put it back in the bottle. Mark a strip of card in centimetres and stick it on the side of the bottle. Leave it outside to collect rain.
How much is in the bottle after drizzle? How much after heavy rain? How much after a downpour?

18

When the sun comes out after a rainstorm, stand with your back to the sun and you may see a **rainbow**.

Sunlight shining through raindrops splits into 7 colours and makes a rainbow in the sky.

Can you see the 7 colours of the rainbow?

 THINK ABOUT IT!

Water on Earth is never lost. It goes round and round. Water falls to Earth from the clouds as rain. As the sun heats water on Earth, it becomes vapour in the air and rises up to form clouds again.

19

Snow and ice

In cold weather, cloud droplets sometimes stay frozen and join together to fall as sleet or snowflakes.

Have you ever played with snowballs or been skiing, tobogganing or even skating in the snow?

Hailstones form in storm clouds. Heavy hailstones can fall very fast so they don't have time to melt before they reach the ground, even in warm weather.

 LOOK AGAIN

Look again at page 9 to see how cold the temperature must be for water to freeze.

When the air is very cold, water turns to **ice**. Dripping water freezes into icicles.

A skin of ice forms on puddles and ponds.

☀ SAFETY WARNING!

Never go on frozen ponds and lakes – the ice may not be strong enough to hold you.

Water vapour in the air freezes and makes frost patterns on windows.

☀ THINK ABOUT IT!

What has to happen to the temperature for snow and ice to melt?

Storms

Air, water droplets and ice crystals swirl around inside giant storm clouds. All this fierce movement makes a kind of **electricity** which we see as lightning.

Sheet lightning flashes in the clouds.

Fork lightning streaks from the clouds to the ground and back again.

Lightning flashes with a crash of thunder. We see lightning before we hear thunder even though they happen at the same time.

 TRY IT OUT!

Stay indoors in a thunderstorm.
Count between the flash of lightning and the crash of thunder.
The higher you have to count the further away the storm is.

22

A hurricane is a swirling mass of wind and rain that forms over the sea. It becomes less fierce when it reaches land, but it can still do terrible damage.

A tornado is a twisting funnel of air reaching from a storm cloud down to the ground. As it races across land it can destroy houses and can even pick up trucks!

THINK ABOUT IT!

Weather forecasters try to warn us before a storm. What could people do to be prepared when they know a storm is on the way?

Around the world

Different parts of the world have different kinds of weather. Some places are hot, some warm and others cold. The kind of weather that a place has is called its **climate**.

The sun's rays shine straight down onto the middle of Earth, making it hot. Rainforests in this part of the world are always warm and wet.

At the North and South Poles the sun's rays are more spread out so it is freezing cold all the year round.

Did you know that Earth does not face the sun directly, but is tilted?
As Earth moves round the sun the half nearest the sun changes over and the **seasons** change. One half is tipped away from the sun and has winter. The half that is tipped towards the sun has summer.

At the same time of year as children in North America are playing in the snow, children in Australia are swimming in the sea.

 **TRY IT OUT!**

Look in the newspaper to find what kind of weather different parts of the world are having today. What is the hottest place? What is the coldest? What other differences can you spot?

25

Weather forecasts

Weather forecasters are people who collect information from weather stations all over the world – even from space – and use it to tell us what weather we will be having.

Facts about the air, wind, temperature, clouds and rainfall are put into computers which can pass information to each other very quickly.

Weather buoys gather information from the sea.

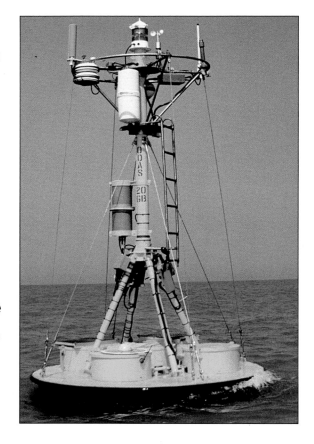

Satellites take pictures of the weather on Earth from space.

 THINK ABOUT IT!

Why do you think farmers, fishermen and pilots need to know what the weather is going to be like?

Farmers used to look for natural signs to help them to forecast the weather. They were not always right. They said that a red sunset meant fine weather the next day, but a red sunrise would bring bad weather. Do you know any other weather sayings?

 TRY IT OUT!

Run your own weather station and record your information on a chart like this. Find out how to collect information about the temperature on page 9, the wind on page 15 and rainfall on page 18. Use page 17 to record what sort of clouds you can see as well. Make a note if it is stormy.

	Temperature	Wind	Clouds	Rainfall	Storms
Monday	17 deg	breezy	white fluffy	0	0
Tuesday					
Wednesday					
Thursday					
Friday					

27

Useful words

Air Air is a mixture of gases we can't see but it is all around us. People and animals need air to breathe.

Atmosphere The atmosphere is a layer of air, dust and tiny droplets of water that surrounds Earth. It helps to keep Earth warm and to protect us from the sun's dangerous rays.

Cirrus Cirrus is the name for fine, wispy clouds that float very high in a blue sky. They warn that the weather is going to change.

Climate Climate is the kind of weather that a place has year after year. For example, places with a temperate climate have warm dry summers and mild winters.

Clouds Clouds are formed when water droplets and ice crystals in the air collect together in a mass. Water falls from clouds as rain, hail or snow.

Crystals Ice crystals are droplets of water frozen into tiny pieces of ice high up in the clouds.

Cumulonimbus Cumulonimbus is the name for giant, towering clouds that bring rain, hail and thunderstorms.

Cumulus Cumulus is the name for small, white fluffy clouds. They are usually seen in fine, sunny weather.

Desert A desert is a dry place where very little rain falls. Some deserts are hot and others are cold. The ground is often rocky or sandy.

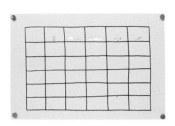

Electricity Electricity is a kind of energy. We use it to power lights, televisions and all kinds of other machines. It is formed naturally inside storm clouds during a thunderstorm.

Ice When the temperature of liquid water drops to below 0 degrees Centigrade it freezes into solid ice.

Mist Mist is cloud that forms near the ground, making it hard to see. A thick mist is called a fog.

Rainbow A rainbow is the bow-shaped arc formed when sunlight shines through raindrops and splits into seven different colours.

Satellite Satellites are a special kind of space craft that circle Earth.

Seasons On certain parts of the Earth, the seasons change through a year from spring, to summer, autumn and winter. Each season has different weather, affecting plants and animals.

Stratus Stratus is the name for layers of very dark low cloud that bring rain.

Temperature The temperature of something is how hot or cold it is. We measure temperature in degrees Centigrade (°C) using a thermometer.

Thermometer We use a thermometer to measure temperature.

Water vapour When water is heated it becomes a gas called water vapour. As water vapour cools, it becomes water again.

Index

About this book

Children are natural scientists. They learn by touching and feeling, noticing, asking questions and trying things out for themselves. The books in the *It's Science!* series are designed for the way children learn. Familiar objects are used as starting points for further learning. *Weather* starts by asking "what's the weather like today?" and explores how and why the weather changes.

Each double page spread introduces a new topic, such as clouds. Information is given, questions asked and activities suggested that encourage children to make discoveries and develop new ideas for themselves. Look out for these panels throughout the book:

TRY IT OUT! indicates a simple activity, using safe materials, that proves or explores a point.
THINK ABOUT IT! indicates a question inspired by the information on the page but which points the reader to areas not covered by the book.
LOOK AGAIN introduces a cross-referencing activity which links themes and facts through the book.

Encourage children not to take the familiar world for granted. Point things out, ask questions and enjoy making scientific discoveries together.